LIGHTNING BOLT BOOKS™

Meet a Baby Hippo

Lisa Owings

Lerner Publications Company

Minneapolis

Content Consultant: Dr. Mark C. Andersen, Department of Fish Wildlife and Conservation Ecology, New Mexico State University

Lerner Publications Company
A division of Lerner Publishing Group, Inc.
241 First Avenue North
Minneapolis, MN 55401 USA

For reading levels and more information, look up this title at www.lernerbooks.com.

Library of Congress Cataloging-in-Publication Data

Owings, Lisa, author.
    Meet a Baby Hippo / Lisa Owings.
        pages cm. — (Lightning Bolt Books™. Baby African animals)
    Audience: 5–8.
    Audience: K to grade 3.
    Includes bibliographical references and index.
    ISBN 978-1-4677-8115-2 (lb : alk. paper) — ISBN 978-1-4677-8363-7 (pb : alk. paper) — ISBN 978-1-4677-8364-4 (EB pdf)
    1. Hippopotamus—Infancy—Juvenile literature. I. Title. II. Title: Meet a Baby Hippo
QL737.U570954 2016
599.63'5139—dc23   2014036683

Manufactured in the United States of America
1 – BP – 7/15/15

Table of Contents

Water Birth

Did you know most baby hippos are born underwater? First, a baby hippo grows in its mother's belly for eight months. Then it is time for the baby to be born.

The mother hippo leaves the herd. She gets ready to have her calf.

Mother hippos find a safe place to give birth.

Soon the mother hippo's baby is born. It swims to the water's surface to breathe.

The calf quickly swims up for its first breath of air!

A baby hippo looks tiny next to its giant mother.

Can you guess the size of a baby hippo? It weighs around 100 pounds (45 kilograms). That is about as heavy as twelve human babies. Adult hippos can weigh up to 8,000 pounds (3,630 kg). That is heavier than two cars!

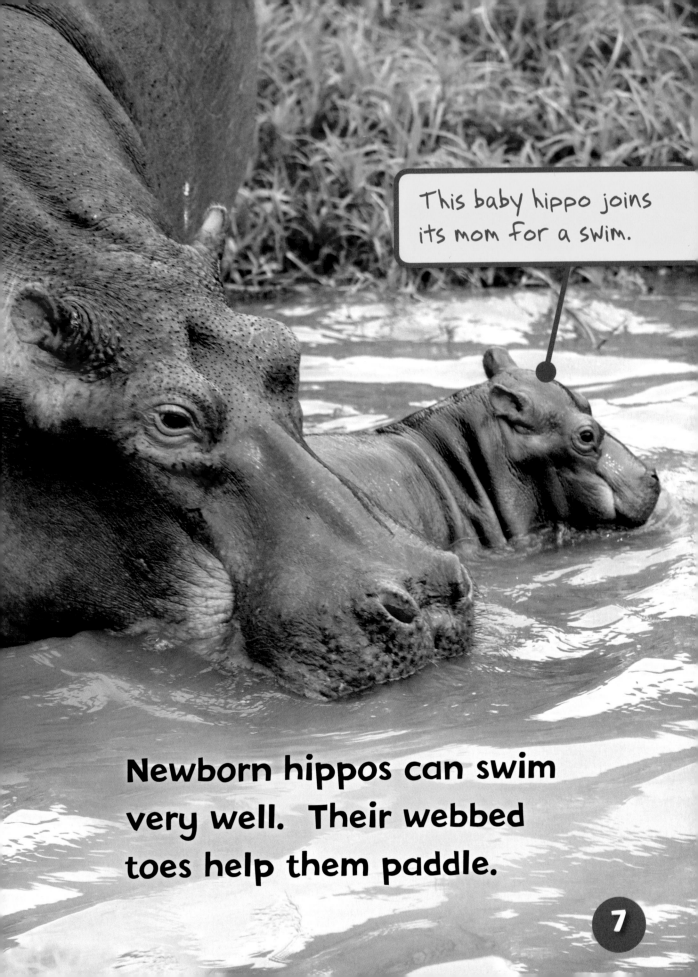

This baby hippo joins its mom for a swim.

Newborn hippos can swim very well. Their webbed toes help them paddle.

Hippo calves are good at diving too.

Their nostrils and ears close to keep the water out.

Hippos cannot stay underwater for more than two minutes.

Hippo calves only spend time with their mothers. Mother hippos do not have help raising the calves.

A mother hippo cares for her calf away from the herd.

9

Learning from Mom

Baby hippos spend most of the day in the water. They splash and swim next to their mothers.

Hippo calves feel at home in the water.

A group of hippos naps in the water.

Swimming is tiring!

Baby hippos climb on their mothers' backs to rest.

Soon the babies get hungry. They dive underwater to nurse. This can be tricky. They must come up for air often.

A baby calf comes up for air after nursing, or drinking milk from its mother.

A baby hippo stays close to its mom. She cleans it with her tongue. She protects it from hungry lions and crocodiles.

Adult hippos block a crocodile from calves.

Mother hippos graze on land at night.

Young babies stay behind in the water for two weeks.

Calves learn to walk on land at about three weeks old.

A herd includes several mothers and young hippos.

Mothers and babies go back to the herd a few weeks after the babies are born. The calves are already getting bigger. They put on several pounds each day!

Grazing and Growing

Its mother's milk is a baby hippo's only food for the first month. The rich milk helps the baby hippo gain weight quickly.

This baby hippo has a lot of growing to do!

Baby hippos learn how to eat grass and other plants by watching their mothers.

After the first month, a baby hippo follows its mother at night. The calf still mainly drinks milk.

Plants are a large part of hippos' diets.

Mothers stop nursing their babies between six and eight months. Then the young hippos eat only plants. Adult hippos eat around 80 pounds (36 kg) of plants per day. Each meal weighs about as much as a large dog.

Older hippo calves may not need their mothers' milk. But they still need protection. Calves stay close to their mothers for five or more years.

A mother looks for any predators coming near the water and her calf.

Making It Big

At six years old, hippos are fully grown. They have become some of the largest animals on Earth.

A hippo's size scares away many predators.

A mother hippo won't leave the water until her calf is strong.

Female hippos begin having babies of their own between seven and fifteen years old. Most have one calf every two years.

Between six and thirteen years old, male hippos begin fighting one another. They open their mouths wide. Only the biggest, strongest male gets to mate.

Can you see the hippos' long teeth?

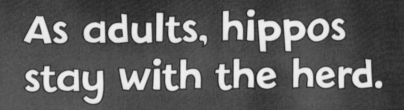

As adults, hippos
stay with the herd.

One male hippo rules the herd.

Other males can stay
in a herd if they don't
fight with the leader.

Adult hippos spend their days relaxing in the water. They move to land when they get cold.

Hot sun keeps these hippos warm.

24

Hippos will walk for miles to find food.

Hippos leave the water at dusk. They spend many hours walking and grazing. Adult hippos do not worry much about predators. They are too big to be a crocodile's lunch!

New baby hippos are born each year.

Hippos mate when the weather is dry. Mothers give birth during the rainy season. Then a new life cycle begins.

Hippos can live forty years or more in the wild. They keep having babies into old age. Each new life brings strength to the herd.

Hippo Life Cycle

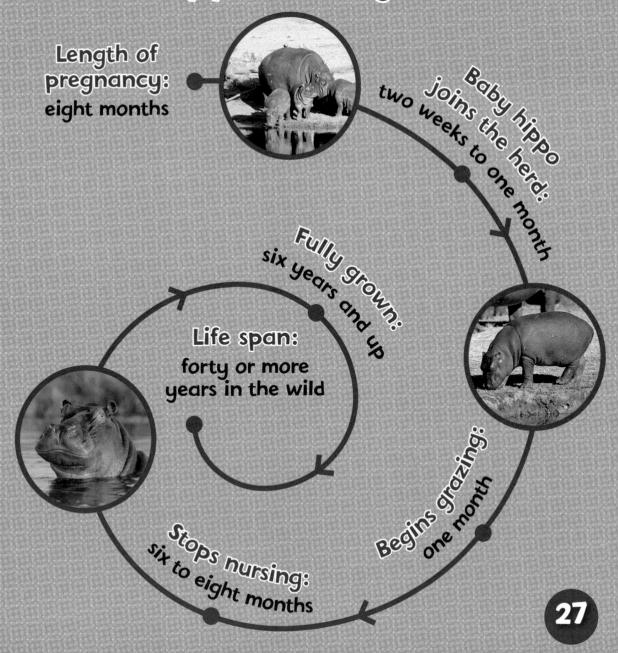

Length of pregnancy: eight months

Baby hippo joins the herd: two weeks to one month

Fully grown: six years and up

Life span: forty or more years in the wild

Begins grazing: one month

Stops nursing: six to eight months

Habitat in Focus

- Hippos spend most of their time in shallow lakes, rivers, or swamps. The water helps them stay cool.

- Hippos eat only grasses and plants that grow near their watery habitats. Sometimes hippos cannot find enough food. They must move to another area.

- People need water for drinking and farming. They take over hippo habitats. But some hippos live in protected areas.

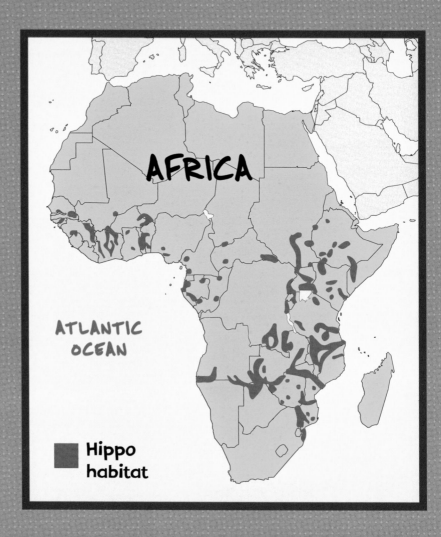

AFRICA

ATLANTIC OCEAN

Hippo habitat

Fun Facts

- *Hippopotamus* means "river horse" in Greek.

- Hippos have an oily pink substance that covers their skin. It protects their skin from the sun.

- Adult hippos cannot swim. They are too heavy! Instead, they walk along the river bottom.

- Hippos may be heavy. But they are fast! They can easily outrun a human on land.

Glossary

calf: a baby hippo

dusk: the time of day when it starts to get dark

graze: to feed on grasses and plants

herd: a group of animals that lives together

mate: to join together to produce young

nurse: to drink milk from a mother

Further Reading

Mattern, Joanne. *Hippos and Rhinos.* Vero Beach, FL: Rourke, 2013.

Nagelhout, Ryan. *Huge Hippos.* New York: Gareth Stevens, 2014.

National Geographic Kids: Hippopotamus http://kids.nationalgeographic.com/content/kids /en_US/animals/hippopotamus

Owens, Henry. *How to Track a Hippo.* New York: Windmill Books, 2014.

PBS Kids: If You Were a Hippopotamus http://pbskids.org/video/?category=Between%20 the%20Lions&pid=3RwPByhjQUvCmr1SfqEhGNdPs sR_hjYq

San Diego Zoo Kids: Hippopotamus http://kids.sandiegozoo.org/animals/mammals /hippopotamus

Index

Photo Acknowledgments

The images in this book are used with the permission of: © Sam Dcruz/Shutterstock Images, pp. 2, 20; © David Northcott/Danita Delimont Photography/Newscom, p. 4; © John James/Mirrorpix/Newscom, p. 5; © Anup Shah/Thinkstock, pp. 6, 26; © Goddard Photography/Thinkstock, p. 7; © Patrick Rolands/Shutterstock Images, p. 8; © Prill/Shutterstock Images, p. 9; © Lucie Caizlova/Thinkstock, p. 10; © Steve Bloom Images/Alamy, p. 11; © Catherine Milton/Thinkstock, p. 12; © John Warburton-Lee Photography/Alamy, p. 13; © EcoPrint/Shutterstock Images, pp. 14, 15, 27 (bottom right); © Mikhail Blajenov/Shutterstock Images, p. 16; © Gerrit de Vries/Shutterstock Images, pp. 17, 27 (bottom left); © Anton Ivanov/Shutterstock Images, pp. 18, 22, 31; © bikeriderlondon/Shutterstock Images, pp. 19, 27 (top); © Gary Stone/Shutterstock Images, p. 21; © Nicolas Poizot/Shutterstock Images, p. 23; © gilya/Shutterstock Images, p. 24; © Serge Vero/Shutterstock Images, p. 25; Red Line Editorial, p. 28; © Hailin Chen/Shutterstock Images, p. 30.

Front cover: © Andrew Yates/AFP/Getty Images.

Main body text set in Johann Light 30/36.